Walk in Beauty:

A Guide to Living in Indigenous Wisdom

Dearest Pat

Love

Alison

By

Alison Dhuanna

Table of Contents

Dedication

To my Muse the humble Blackbird, thank you.

Acknowledgements

I would like to acknowledge the influence of the Haiku Poet Basho in my writing of this book and also the late Author John O Donahue whose words about Beauty helped me to see its' universal value for others and get it published. Thank you to my beloved partner Jay who is so much part of the adventure.

About the Author

Alison Dhuanna is an Astrologer, Writer and Artist living in Hebden Bridge in West Yorkshire. She was born in Johannesburg coming to England in 1988 to study. She did a degree including Creative Writing through the Open University receiving a distinction for Poetry and Creative Writing. The situation of her upbringing led to her being diagnosed with PTSD and it took many years of recovery to emerge from this. She is a Professional Astrologer for some 25 years, sharing the stories of the stars and nature.

Chapter One: Stripping Away Complexity

In the early spring of 2018 I began walking as if I had suddenly grown winged sandals. At the same time I began to write Haikus wanting to capture those special moments that arose each day. Before long a book crossed my path called Narrow Path to the Interior and other writings by Matsuo Basho. This work from the 6th century is a travelogue of haiku poems and it greatly encouraged me to master this form which I continue to do. My process has been very simple, to walk and write every day. To notice the simple detail and elegance of a moment that has energy and power, and share it with you the reader.

A book of poetry came together from that year which seemed to encompass a new emerging sense of purpose and perhaps the clearest experience I had of piercing ever deeper into another reality which I came to understand as Holographic. In a nutshell the same things will appear periodically on your journey, so look out for them.

Some four years after writing the book at the beginning of the Russia Ukraine war I listened to a podcast by John O'Donahue on the On Being Project, one of the last interviews he gave before his sudden death in 2008. It was entitled The Inner Landscape of Beauty and suddenly in that moment I realised the profound experience I had was also of value to other people and I determined to create a version of that raw material comprising many hundreds of haikus as a guide book to opening this place within ourselves. Part of my realisation was that if more people lived in this reality of 'Beauty' there would no longer be wars and environmental disaster. A great tenderness get holds of the heart until one's love and celebration of life swills over and over.

I live in a beautiful place in the Pennines called Hebden Bridge in West Yorkshire which forms the palette of many of my walks. The years journeys took me as far afield as the Outer Hebrides and back again, like a stone falling into a pond rippling to the outer edges of the British isles and then returning to the centre. Most of the walks took place with my two dogs Lily who is a Jack Russel and Bongo a Yorkshire terrier.

The Haikus soon became a part of my internal rhythm and their simplicity has been a transformation of my way of being and communicating. It became a spiritual discipline in a world of endless communications; to be still, succinct and simple. As I sit down to revamp this book I realise it is the same time of spring – the dandelions are all just beginning to flower again.

Overnight, bare trees
Adorned by leafy garment;
A thousand green shades

The song of the thrush
And the tits
pierce through the woodland

The full moon has urged
Dandelions to bloom;
Yellow way markers

One hundred chapels;
A valley of revolution,
Wild non-conformists.

Beneath the blossoming trees
A brooch of dazzling flowers;
Three ravens overhead.

In a silent glade
Mass spines of a dragon
Are dreaming with me.

We climb out of the valley
Intoxicated by sky;
The expanse of moor

Grey geese rearing
Forty goslings between them
Orange beaks so bright.

Is there a place for me
In the family of things?
The cause of my suffering.

After a few months of writing there was a moment of epiphany one day as I saw the blackbird – and I mean really saw it. I have seen many blackbirds but to this day I realise I hadn't really seen them properly. This day I said a prayer to Mother Earth to teach me and within minutes I had this encounter with the blackbird. Its eye pierced into my soul. I stood there my heart broken open, crying as I perceived the wonder of this perfect little bird being, and through it the wonder of the whole of creation

An invitation to Earth;

Speak through my creative soul'
Teach me thou mysteries;

Blackbird alights here
Her shocking yellow eye
Beckons me to "see";

A wondrous garden,
Curved walls created in stone
Cherry plums blossom;

An arch of gritstone
Supports the winding river
As she emerges;

Two doves bank above
Gazing at the sparkling sun;
Here lives the Holy Spirit

There are a few things that strike me on reflection that I invite you to bring into your own life and begin this practice. I wrote Haiku - it is an easy form of poetry to get the hang of and after a time I noticed the simple rhythm of it was creating a rhythm in my brain and body. I literally started thinking in haikus without having to think! Haiku has a rhythm of 5 – 7 – 5 syllables.

However, that said any creative process would work so if you are more inclined to do this with journalling, art or photography then do that – whatever makes it doable and exciting for you.

Make a commitment to regular walking through all the seasons and to keep it going for a whole cycle of nature. This commitment and patience are important. The encounter with Blackbird came around a month into my walks and it began an opening of seeing deeper and deeper into the beauty of things. Ordinary things, things that may not even be beautiful to anyone else like geese hissing on the narrow canal path.

I didn't take a pen and paper with me as I didn't want my walk to be disrupted by writing, plus I had two small terriers who love to yap and snarl at any passing dogs. I determined that if it was a vivid enough experience I would still remember it when I got home and this worked well because probably I would have written around twice as many haikus taking the pen with me. My suggestion is to go walking with as much presence as possible. Still often on a walk I am some way in and realise I haven't seen a thing I'm so lost in conversations and to do lists in my head! It takes patience to rewire ourselves into Presence – we are deconditioning many layers of ways we have been taught to think that took us out of a loving relationship with the land.

Where I live for example, there used to be many weavers in their cottages connected to the sheep that provided the wool, the land and their work was artisan in nature. With industrialisation these people were pulled into the mills, even the children were set to work creating wealth for a few. It is always such a great pleasure to me that Hebden Bridge now celebrates creativity once more and many artists and writers come to live here. It is in a sense the recovery of a whole way of living and being that once was very natural to our ancestors.

These days many of us including myself spend a lot of time on computers and in zoom rooms. This simple practice is a balance to that technological ways of living and develops other parts of the brain and helps us to be embodied. It is through being embodied we find our core stability and a deeper sense of security beyond identity, money and stuff; it is a highly beneficial state to live in for emotional and physical health. When I was 18 years old I was diagnosed as having PTSD and I have struggled with mental health problems my whole life. It is through this discovery of the Landscape of Inner Beauty that my life has become enriched and brings daily bursts of joy and even ecstasy.

Dandelions await
in perfect symmetry
A fresh blast of wind;

Geese hiss as we pass;
Young beneath protective wings
With giant webbed feet.

Sunlight drenches the
Canopy of the woods

Awash with birdsong.
Rush of ravens wing
Reminds me; I am part of
The human family;

Bees around Elder;
Glistening flowers open
For a tea ritual;

Baubles of pure white
Hawthorne's perfume halts me
-      Intoxicating;

Bride of a Prince;
Black Dove, messenger of peace
Dawn of a New Earth.

In the secret garden,
New hives of mountain bees where
The keepers gather.

The Beekeeper with
his hat and smoking vessel,
inspects new hives.

Chapter Two: After the Swallows Came

We saw the first swallows in late May that year as we drove to Bradford from the Calder Valley. Living here in deep geological crevices formed in the Ice Age, one can get valley fever and there is always a sense of liberation as one reaches the higher ground and spaciousness of the moorland.

The first two swallows
Have arrived in Yorkshire
To rapturous applause.

The laburnum with her
Bright acid yellow flowers
Dangles over walls;

The swifts are swooping;
Joy of their long migration
Over for now.

Walking along the canal in the summer there is a diversity of nature experiences, but also people. I find most days I'm not as interested in people as nature but sometimes the field of human experience catches my attention. I reflected a lot on this – why did it take me so long to notice the beauty of humans? Looking back through the poems people had caught my eye like the bee keepers and yet in some deep way I had cut off from this human beauty.

I mentioned earlier in the book that I had PTSD as a young person and it took me a long time to recover with a number of breakdowns over the years. As a child growing up under Apartheid I had witnessed the worst that human beings could do to each other to secure their power and wealth, and although I would say I'm a natural optimist by nature, it has been such a process to integrate this totality of human experience. That we could on the once hand

be so easily manipulated, be so prone to violence when our space
is threatened and yet also have the potential for so much love and
goodness.

Tan linen trousers,
Navy blue tie and jacket
And a straw bowler hat.

Three quarter old jeans
Soft footfall of his flip flops;
A canal dweller.

Catkins smother paths
Form big clumps in the canal,
Seeking seeding places.

Harlequin yellow
And boats of many colours,
Moored here for summer.

A walk in Hardcastle Craggs, National Trust property is one of the
highlights of living in Hebden Bridge. Leaving my friend, who has
recently had a knee replacement, to paint the river, I set off on the
rail track walk from Gibson's Mill.

Clumps of wild garlic,
Thick and pungent aroma
Edge the woodland path;

A black Labrador
Deftly plucks pheasants feather
From my surprised hand;

Lightness arises
Amidst the violet bluebells
And wood anenomes;

Back to my daily walk past St James the Great church and into Colden Clough. I never get bored of this walk as nature daily provides new moments of tender beauty.

In this symphony
Of birds, it's impossible
To see them through the trees;

Why does the doves song
Pull at my heart strings?
Evoking sadness;

A rush of pure white
Wings through a crown of jewels;
Dove flies free above.

Oak has unfurled her
Soft, lime green leaves;
Scalloped perfection.

Another of my favourite walks when I am tired and don't fancy the hills is along the canal to Callas Bridge. The houses that lie between the river and the canal hold a fascination for me. These are brave dwellers in a place that frequently floods. Their houses somehow seem brighter than others though as if the ever present danger of the river has brought them alive.

On reflection the entire process I experienced that year brought me closer to living and being like Indigenous people, in these islands the Celts and Norse people were very much connected and saw the natural intelligence of nature. I'm feeling though also an awakening in my predominently English DNA. Experiencing these simple pleasures of life I noticed how my constant and gnawing disatisfaction with my life and myself was dropping away and I was more and more in a space of inner bliss communing with birds, flowers and plants and coming online more and more human beings.

Gay azaeleas,
Magnolia, clematis
Pour over the fence;

Stream from the woodland
Cascades over Millstone Grit
Into the canal;

A rush of chaffinch
Before my very nose flies
With her two dear friends;

A flash of colour;
The kingfisher vanishes
Into the undergrowth;

Was it a Goldcrest
So rare and small that I saw?
All my hearts' desire.

Chapter Three: Journey to the Outer Hebrides

In late summer we set off for Lewis in the Outer Hebrides at the invitation of our friends Karen and Ron with great excitement, having always wanted to visit these remote islands. It seems almost an enchanted place, the summer isles of mythical Selkie legends. Suddenly the vista of beauty expanded from our small beautiful valley outwards to the furtherest edges of the United Kingdom. The landscape we drove through to get there was some of the most extraordinary I have seen, a real feast for the senses.

Swept into Scotland
In the arms of storm Hector,
Trees swirl like confetti;

Waterfalls thunder
Down magnificent mountains
Of Argyll and Bute;

Saturated light
Aches to become a rainbow,
Clinging to Glencoe;

Five Sisters of Kintail
Released their turbulent tears
To the loch below

At Eileen Donan
The eagle circles overhead,
chased off by sea gulls.

At the outer edge
Of the sacred isles of Lewis,
The ocean rolls in.
Where two streams meet the sea,

The shrikes sing their wild song
Lifted on the wind;

Seven seals frolic
Beyond the Lewisian gneiss
In the turquoise ocean;

Pink orchids glazed with
Buttercups and white clover;
Cry of the artic terns;

Black headed gulls bounce
Above the thrilling waves,
Round barely clad women.

The exquisite thrill
As the gannet fold hers wings,
Splash! She disappears.

The fulmer parents
Sit watchfully upon nests,
Sheltered by black rocks;

In gongs and chimes
The voice of the well maidens
Echoes eternity;

Where the river meets
the ocean, yellow irises;
A rich, fertile place;

The black houses at dusk
Slope gently towards the sea,
Illuminated;

Solstice at Callanish

Bag pipes and drums, the horn sounds;
A celebration

Within the Earth's core
Explosions of Cygnus's light
in the deep caverns.

Yellow irises,

Vibrant heather, peachy rocks
Harris tweed palette;

The eagle led us
To ponds of waterlilies
Between the mountains;

From our cosy yurt
'Hag' mountain overlooks us;
She speaks to my heart

Meeting with old friends
Moet, chips and scallop balls;
Endings and beginnings.

The cuckoos strange song
In the Garden of Eden,
Time is returning.

Silent serenity;
The Five Sisters of Kintail
Deeply at rest now.

Chapter Four: A Glorious Summer

We returned home a week after the summer solstice to beautiful weather in Hebden Bridge. The summer seems endless this year. Sometimes you return from holiday and feel depressed getting back to normal life. How wonderful to live in a place which has the perpetual feeling of being on holiday, even when one is working. True vocation never feels quite like work.

Walking along by Salem Fields there are many people out walking and paddling in the river. I see in my reality people enjoying nature and I want to invite you reading this book to enjoy it more, see it even more.

Young people soaking
In the river in summer,
In their secret world.

I walk to St John in Wilderness on Sunday morning as our ancestors would have done. A sign tells me that Charles Wesley the famous preacher and hymn writer passed this way too.

Voluptuous trees
And sensual river rocks;
Wrens singing their songs;

At Hoo Hole Charles Wesley
Gave a rousing sermon
Beneath an old tree;

Our voices raise up
'A Thousand Tongues to Sing'
To the wild Pennines.

It's so hot it reminds me of my childhood years ago in Johannesburg where I grew up. I'm taking myself and dogs paddling every day.

Summer at Jack Bridge;
Dogs paddling, tadpoles lounging
Shimmering water;

The dragon's lair
hidden beneath foliage;
Baby black birds' home.

Fish languishing at
Lock Nine's tepid waters
in afternoon sun;

At Lock Eleven,
Young geese learn the art
Of preening their wings.

In the winter I visited a beautiful spot by the river near Horsehold and I wanted to come back here in the summer to swim. Today in early July I set off with my dogs, Bongo and Lily. I also have Oreo my neighbours Shi Tzu.

Hauling me upwards,
Lily, Bongo, Oreo
Like sled dogs scamper;

Ancient beech woods
Their serpent roots, a fire pit,
But now all is still.

Sounds of the river
And the blessed shade of leaves

Spur us down the hill;
When I first came upon this place from the other direction I had a spontaneous vision of people, perhaps in the olden days, doing baptisms here. John the Baptist did his baptisms at Bethany a place where about 4 springs met. I stop to count and there are also 4 streams here forming a larger 5th river cascading through the woods. If you clamber downstream there is a deeper pool where I was able to totally immerse myself.

The thrill of cold water
And grit stone beneath my feet,
In full submersion;

Gathering Gaia's dreams;
Blessed beyond limitations
Droplets of pure light.

The dogs have different responses to the river. Bongo used to be afraid of water, but now he loves to come in with me. He follows me to the deep pool sticking his head right underwater to pick up oversized stones in his small mouth. Lily doesn't like water at all, but she gets in to make sure she can keep an eye on me. She skips from rock to rock to ensure she doesn't lose her visual of what I am doing. Oreo is the youngest and still unsure of herself. She isn't as agile as the other two, designed as a temple dog by her ancestry. She is happy to cool off in the shallow stream drenching her thick fur. When I scramble back upstream she is there by my bag and clothes having soaked them nicely for me.

Walking through the woods
In an old, blue worn swimsuit
And soggy sandals;

I dry myself off;
Lounging on leafy woodland,
Sticks flying in the sun.

I am enjoying lying in the sun drying off, but the dogs hear another dog barking and set off a cacophony of sound. Little dogs with big voices echoing through the valley. I put my clothes back on and head for home.

I often walk down the canal path towards Hebden Bridge town and have a great affinity with the birds who live there. I feel them to be part of our living community more and more as my brain is being rewired to see beauty by the writing of these haikus. There are a number of groups who tend to live separately: Canada geese and Mallard ducks are the largest groups. There is a smaller group of white geese and Aylesbury ducks. I follow the well-being of the young ones as if they were my own and always feel upset to notice some disappear. This is the way of nature and I know that. If they all survived there would be too many and the canal and river couldn't support them. Still it upsets me and I feel for the mother's keeping their young safe in the perilous environment.

In the past few weeks a white goose who is living alone keeps catching my attention. Nature is a great healer to call attention to that which troubles the human mind, and being excluded is perhaps our greatest fear. I perceive her to be ill. Her feathers don't look good and she is a bit muddy around one leg. Usually birds are very good at keeping their feathers clean. I say many prayers for her as I pass by. Still she lives apart but I notice a bit more vitality in her step.

We smell the rain, feel
subtle changes in pressure
before it came down.

England has sold out
Of Gareth Southgate waist coats;
A national joy.

Today I planted
'Love Parade' achillea
On our council estate.

17

Flowers change the world
Bring happiness in poverty,
Everyone can see.

What I love about this area is there are infinite beautiful walks.
Today I set off from the a camping field at Cragg Vale down Hoo
Hole Lane to walk back to Hebden Bridge. It was a very steep
climb, so not for the faint hearted.

Climbing the steep hill,
boots imprint dusty roots
in a pine forest;

White moths arising,
puffs of smoke from spiky grass
as we pass them by;

Burnt Sienna and
lime bilberry leaves, withered
by the scorching sun;

Mgical forest
of Rowan, Birch and Oak trees;
comfort in the sun;

A handful of bilberries
for a thirsty mouth
is blissful relief.

The time of the harvest has arrived, the ripening of nature. I have
moved through this process of writing haikus each day in Spring
and Summer and now we are right on the edge of Autumn. I feel I
have changed and I am much more peaceful and relaxed. I see
around me everywhere people stressed in another reality of linear
time, pressure and expectation. I want them to join me over here in
the Garden of Eden but I'm not sure how to communicate that.

Night sky indigo;
Phallic fronds of buddleah
Tantalising butterflies;

Juicy raspberries
Rich red on the tongue;
Sweetness and sharpness.

The first blackberries
So tart on the tongue;
The wildest harvest.

How soft the butterfly;
White wings hover over heart
Healing its hardness.

Chapter Five – Return to Eden

We decided spontaneously to take a journey north in our Bedford Rascal camper van Ursula before the cold months returned. I had read recently about the River Eden travelling from south to north and felt a calling to its waters. I also wanted to walk some of the Pennine Way in the far north above Hadrian's Wall.

From Hebden Bridge to
The Eden Valley river,
The pilgrimage begins;

Dragons are dancing
Among the pink, wispy clouds
In the dawning day;

Two swans rest peacefully
Beneath the motorway bridge;
Affirming of life.

Our first stop is at Long Meg and her Daughters, a large stone circle in the Eden Valley. Arriving early in the morning, we eat our breakfast picnic style on a large stone before wondering around. It is 26th July 2018, Red Cosmic Moon Galactic New Year in the Mayan calendar.

The two doves of Eros
Announced our arrival
In Eden Valley;

My morning pages
And dandelion coffee
Beneath the Ash at Long Meg;

Mother buzzard teaches
Her screeching young to fly
Twix stones and mountains;

We set of to visit St Peter's Church in Dacre via Penrith and the
Seat of Arthur. Penrith is chaotic as there is a music festival on.
We are glad to get to the peace of St Peter's and eager to see the
four Pole Star Bears we have seen pictures of in The Spine of
Albion by Gary Bitcliffe and Caroline Hoar.

In an ancient church
The buzzard sits patiently
Upon an old grave;

Four Bears hold pillars
Connecting Heaven and Earth,
In Dacre churchyard;

Entering the space
between two immortal trees,
I find stillness;

St Geo George
Looking quite like Joan of Arc
Upon a dragon;

A stained glass window
Reveals the serpent climbing
The Tree of Knowledge.

We figured out the best place to reach the river Eden was at
Armathwaite, so in the late afternoon we went for a swim.

Fear grips me as I
Sink into the strong currents
Of river Eden;

Travelling with force
From South to North, relentless
You journey your way;

Clinging onto moss
And rock, hundreds of minnows
Are baptised with me;

Seven horses came
To drink at the waters' edge
In the cool evening.

Pied wagtail inspects
The campsite round about
With bobbing tail;

Bees buzz above us
Pollinating an old Lime
With ambient hum;

Doves coo their love song,
From the branches above,
Over our camper;

A red sun setting
Whilst storm clouds gather overhead;
Rumbles of thunder.

Chapter Six: Initiation

It rained throughout the night and I dreamt that I was doing a Rite of Passage into womanhood with a friend's daughter. Rites of Passage for young and older people are something else we have lost touch with in our industrialised society that I feel would help us become more stable if we reintroduced them.

Tree dancing shadows
Adorn the awning at dawn
Welcoming the day;

Woodpecker beats out rythms
Our eyes search the foliage
To catch sight of her;

The Red Stone cliffs
Folding and furling around me;
Watched by water spirits;

Within the red cloak
of the Earthly Troubadour
I am enclosed.

After an incredible walk along the sandstone cliffs of the Eden river, I felt myself become a Red Troubadour in the cloak of Mother Earth. It was a powerful initiation, a mystical experience that even years on I feel as if it happened yesterday. Later I came to see it as an initiation connected to the Mary Magdalen Troubadour tradition.

We set off to Wreay to visit a church built by a woman called Sarah Losh after the death of her sister. The journey has taken on a holographic feel, how many dimensions are we inhabiting?

A beautiful church
Created by a woman
For her dead sister;

Exotic designs
In alabaster and oak
From all her travels.

At Carlisle Cathedral
We search for kissing dragons
In an arc of stars.

The following morning we awake to the day that the longest Total Lunar Eclipse this century will take place. In the early morning I heard the unusual cry of a bird and these words came to me.

I heard a strangers voice
One I did not understand

In the Garden of Eden;
At first it was a plaintive cry
But still I listened carefully,
Sure it had its own unique tone
And its own certain place.

In the family of birds
Each has its own song and rhythm
With no need to try to be like another.
Their clear voices ring straight from their beings
And each morning their chorus rises with the sun
Brings new life, new purpose;
Once more I heard the strangers voice.

Black Moss pools are still;
Weaving paths through woods, awaiting
A lunar eclipse;

Horse tails reflected
The smell of the pine forest,
Dead trees in the water;

Faeries with teeth,
Huge footprints of a were wolf
alarm us humans;

The rain has fallen
The air fresh, pine needles drenched;
The earth is nourished;

As the wind shakes the trees
Large goblets rain down on us
Causing much laughter

At 8.30pm I walked to the road alone to watch the eclipse as we
are surrounded by trees at the campsite. The moon is due to rise in
the South West and it will already be eclipsing. Dark storm clouds
are gathering and I start to feel a bit uneasy standing beneath a
huge chestnut tree as I sense the lightening is imminent.

Following the cries
Of the fledgling buzzard
I witness her flight

Chased by a black storm
Thunder and lightening flashes
Hide the moon's eclipse

After a dramatic eclipse in which approximately 90.000 lightening
strikes took place in Britain and I was outside in it almost running
to get away from where I perceived the storm might strike. I didn't
see the lunar eclipse but I certainly felt it. We set off further north
to Hadrian's wall and the wilderness of Northumberland beyond.
We notice in the small village of Simonburn they are having a fete
and dog show. The rain has stopped just in time.

Raspberry jam, wild
Garlic, dandelion
Syrup at Simonburn fete

The weather worsens though with predicted high winds and our
campsite tonight is exposed on top of a hill.

Battling with high winds
I cling to the camper van
The tent whipping around

The following day we spend the entire day in the campervan with the dogs. We don't dare move Ursula in the high winds. I have time to absorb and contemplate the events of the journey. It was quite incredible to see two lots of fledgling buzzards in two days. In my mind it is emerging that we are in a Rubedo phase of alchemy as humanity. Rubedo means 'conjunction' and the Red Phoenix appears as a symbol. This red phase of alchemy begins with the Alchemical Wedding of the Sun and the Moon which is an eclipse. On their wedding night the vessel is heated to increase their passion and the two become one in the fires of love which was the incredible amount of lightening strikes. As fixed Philosophic Sulphur and volatile Philosophic Mercury unite, matter dries completely and becomes a bright, red powder. Within this intense fire of passion they conceive their child The Philosophers Stone. We all have within us a Philosopher's Stone which is the perfect fractal of self. The perfect reflection of self is our unique tone or voice created in resonance in our body.

Finally at 5pm the rain eases off and we emerge into the fresh air.

Roan white calves
Ancesters of Boanna
Leap across the grass

That night we have clear skies and a most welcome sight of the milky way in the darkness of this wild place.

Dancing beneath Cygnus
The red moon, Ursa and Mars
Strange songs on my tongue

Chapter Seven: Medicine Walk to Coventina's Well

The following day we set off a day early to come home as the weather is still very windy. I'm going to do a medicine walk though along what is called the Pennine Experience to the Well of Coventina at the Mithras Temple, Hadrians Wall. At Coventina's Well Mimulus flowers surround it. Dr Bach found the Mimulus flower excellent to help fear.

You can do your own Medicine Walk of any length by creating an intention and then being very present and noticing what happens. You may surprise yourself in how you will instinctively know the meaning of plants, animals and events on your walk. Through regular Medicine Walks you will effortlessly awaken sleeping gifts in your DNA and know at the deepest level how much you are loved and that we are all connected in the Web of Life.

The medicine walk begins
With the cry of buzzard
To Coventina's Well

Perilous journey
A labyrinth of sharp thistles
Clutching my two dogs

The sheep show the way
Up their invisible trail
Of ancient Elder

Lost in the wilderness
I find my bearing through woods
I see on my map

Crossing the small stream
Of flowing goodness
My doubts are settled

Puffs of small white moths
Rise from the damp grass where our
Gentle footsteps pass

At the edge of woods
I breath deeply the smell
Of the sticky cones

Songs from Boanna
The sacred cow, and Epona
The horse, now flow

Horses stop grazing
Curious at the song
Praising their ancestors

A path of Rowan
Orange berries and sweetgrass
Dazzling the senses

Over bubbling brook
And flowering meadows
Sun on our faces

Meeting my beloved
We drink at the well together
with yellow flowers

A moment of love
Shared with a French woman
who speaks perfect 'sheep'.

The Mithras Temple
Of the Sacred Black Bull marks
a strange Sun Goddess

Chapter Eight - Rite of Passage

Having returned home early due to the weather, my partner suggested I walk the next part of the Pennine Way from the White House at Blackstone Edge to Hebden Bridge where we live. I feel I have experienced a meeting of inner Eden with outer Eden and the holographic universe has opened up to me in a new way in the last few days. It feels like the perfect day to do this pilgrimage, returning home.

From Blackstone Edge
I am returning to my home;
Quirky Hebden Bridge

A Fool with her dog
A knapsack of nourishment
We walk heart to heart

Along the reservoirs
White, red and black silt revealed
In depleted pools

With a cry Falcoln
Soars into the sky
With her new fledgling

Stone dragon arises
From the Backbone of Britain
Revealing presence

Flocks of small birds
Arise from the sedge grass
Awash with sweet songs

At Stoodley Pike wild
And dark presence of clouds;
A gentle man lunching

Down the valley home
Tired feet and happy heart
Through lush woodland stroll

Children in canal
Laughing on a dingy boat
Welcome me back home

You may recall that at Long Meg and her daughter's stone circle I had a dream where I was doing a Rite of Passage with a friend's daughter. Like many young women today she is struggling at school with the many pressures of exams, friendships and social media and so I have offered her and her mum the opportunity to go for this walk.

Gathered at the Cross
Kestrel swoops in to show us;
Its' time to begin

Young girl leads the way
Her footfall becomes more sure
As we journey on

A small white horse came
Straight to her gentle hands
Along with a brave fly

Heather is blooming
Medicine of belonging
In its purple haze

The deer springs across
Our path through a field of reeds;
She protects her young

A single dove sits atop
An enormous pine
Like a Christmas Tree

The darting swallows
Travellers from Africa;
Pilots of repute

Three skylarks
Bobbing across the evening
Sky of pinky light

We plunge together
Into the sacred red pool
Beneath the pine trees

Her Mother gathers
A medicine bag of reeds;
A buzzards feather

Sunset of gold light
Seeps through the trees, shapes the rocks
of the Great Bride Stones

Silently the owl
Looks deeply into our eyes
As it circles round

Through narrow passage
Of two mossy rocks we squeeze
Into a new life

Standing on the last
Mountain lit by the sun
At its pinnacle

A new crescent moon
A pomegranate shared by
mother and daughter

Chapter Nine: Life as a Prayer

In the last few days it as if I am seeing things for the first time again. I find myself transfixed to a tree or a flock of birds. I felt as if I suddenly saw this tree full of flowers and like the blackbird so many months before it brough tears and heart opening. How could I not have noticed its exquisite beauty before even though I had walked past it many times?

A new level of noticing and appreciating life has awoken in me. It seems that every walk has become a prayer for the earth and water to be healed. Could it be that every act is also becoming a prayer? I invite you the reader to become a troubadour, a pilgrim and celebrator of life. If there were enough of us living this way big changes would happen and I feel that is the path ahead. I have written this book as part of an evolutionary moment, the fulfilment of a New Heaven, New Earth prophecy. Its not a different place, its a different perspective.

The rush of a flock
Of ravens wings above me
Brings tears to my eyes

Squawking geese trapped in
The low lock water rescued
By a gentleman
(eating breakfast)

Of all the trees
The berries of the Rowan
Are most glorious

The geese are now free
A synthesis of movement
And infinite grace

His knapsack and large
Umbrella strapped to his
Upright striding form

In the Autumn we decided to go and spend a week with our friends
in Frome, Somerset. It's our first journey down South since our life
changing pilgrimage along the St Mary and Michael ley lines last
summer so it brings back many happy memories. We share a
distinct feeling that we have been living 'out of time' as it seems
that it was all a long time ago.

The towering rocks
Of Cheddar Gorge twist and turn
Clothed in wildest thyme

At the Church of St John in Axebridge

Hear a miracle!
An Angel Dove of the Lord
Healed a broken heart

Two mermaids flanking
Our Lady in deep prayer;
The Annunciation

A choir of voices
Rose high in Wells Cathedral
Brought tears to our eyes

The ancient clock strikes
Four, above our Beloved's head;
Time for seeds to fall

The kind chaplain points
to Our Lady dressed in green
beneath a fertile cross

The Immortal Yew
And Seven Wells heard our prayer
For the Church of Our Lord

Choirs of voices rose
Gazing deep into layers
Of translucent waters

Yellow Sandstone brick
Has made cities of gold
A promised land

Mother swan and her
Downey cygnets preen beneath
The weeping willow

A single white dove
Patiently awaits entrance
To Bishops Palace

May the pelican
Who pecks her own heart for love
Of her young draw near

Encircling Brides Mound
Singing to young maidens
And the Blessed Grail

The Blue cup appears
Hovering in my hands
As I pray for renewal

After hearing a beautiful sung Eucharist at Edington Priory, Wiltshire I walk back from the White horse of Westbury to Frome Somerset, some ten miles with my friend Adam who is a seasoned walker.

From the Westbury
White Horse we tread the edge
Of Salisbury plain

The gentle curves of Wiltshire
Stretch out before us
Laced with rare flowers

Cley Hill our distant
Magical beacon rising
Up from the green land

Rich red cows grazing
The finest grass of England;
Handsome bulls close by

Through the magical woods
Our voices sing to Elen
And to the shy deer

Into the cows mud
My sandal disappears
Sucked into the wet

Approaching Frome a
White egret flies before us
In the sky at dusk

The next day we visit the Frome river.

The delicate song
Of the river over shale;
Washer at the Ford

Talking in the roots
Of the tree by the river
In the pleasant shade

Two white doves soaring
High winds catch their wings
Banking above us

The She Chestnut tree
Offers her spiky lime fruit
To our Father Sun

On our return journey to Yorkshire made in the early morning we
see many rainbows

From the cloud dragons
Gaping jaws a pearl of light
Falling from heaven

Back home and there is definitely a change in the seasons

A chill in the air
And torrents of welcome rain
Have filled the river

The first fallen leaves
Intricate in their design
And autumn colour

In the Autumn we had the opportunity to return for 7 weeks to the
Outer Hebrides. On our first visit I had felt the presence of the
Creator so strongly in that place. I immersed myself completely in

the storms at the North Western point of Lewis coming in off the Atlantic. I felt a strong urge to paint in this period and my haiku's seemed naturally to transform into a visual form. So this book came to a natural conclusion, earlier than I expected. Everything has its own season. What has stayed with me is the inner rhythm this practice imbued into my body, writing just what I recalled after my walks each day. It took me deeply into other dimensions and I hope that these will reveal themselves to the reader as they did to me for they cannot be adequately captured in words. I end with a few Haiku's which capture the profound sense of beauty simply noticing has brought me, and with deepest gratitude I thank Mother Nature my muse.

Moved to tears I see
As if for the first time
The graceful magpie

In rapture I stand
Staring at bright yellow leaves
Now ready to fall

White berries are all
That is left upon the bush,
Winter is sleeping